Half Day Hikes
(Or Less!)

Big Bend Ranch State Park

TEXAS

D1546414

Robert and Jenny Fuller

Half Day
H·I·K·E·S

www.halfdayhikes.com

HALF DAY HIKES Guidebook Series
Copyright © 2019 by Half Day Hikes

First Printing: 2019

Maps by Mettja Kuna, Homegrown Maps, mettja@homegrownmaps.com
Book design by Elena Reznikova, DTPerfect.com

Half Day Hikes (Or Less!) Big Bend Ranch State Park, TX

ISBN 978-1-7330824-0-2 (paperback)

Contacting the Publisher
We welcome feedback on this guide and appreciate if you could advise us of any errors, omissions or interesting facts that could be added in subsequent revisions. Your support will enable a better experience for future users of this guide. Please send feedback to **info@halfdayhikes.com.**

All images © Robert and Jenny Fuller
Front Cover Photo: Closed Canyon
Back Cover Photo: Hoodoos

Printed in the United States of America
Published by Half Day Hikes

info@halfdayhikes.com

Non-Liability Statement: Every effort has been made to ensure the accuracy of the information contained in this guidebook. However, discrepancies may exist and neither the authors nor publisher is responsible for any erroneous information. Hiking in such a remote area is a high-risk activity due to trail condition changes, extreme heat, flash flooding, and other dangers that may be encountered. The readers of this guidebook assume full responsibility for their own safety, hiking preparedness and evaluating personal abilities. The authors and the publisher hereby expressly disclaim any liability for death, injury, accident, or loss associated with or resulting from the use or misuse of the information in this guidebook.

Half Day Hikes (Or Less!)
Big Bend Ranch State Park, Texas

If you've always wanted to explore Big Bend Ranch State Park but didn't know where to start, this guidebook is for you!

Exploring the largest state park in Texas and one of the most remote locations in the entire country may seem daunting, but we've come up with the perfect solution.

This guidebook is a pocket-sized yet informative "trail buddy" to carry with you on the trail, together with a compass and map of the area.

There are so many wonderful experiences and interesting sights to be found in Big Bend Ranch State Park, which is why it's important to take this guidebook along. It's chock-full of hiking tips, maps, highlights, reference points, trailhead directions, and full-color photos depicting trail features to plan and select a hike that's right for you.

The Introduction and Safety Tips section contain essential information associated with visiting such a remote location, and are a must-read prior to your visit.

All of the hikes are easy to moderate in complexity and range in length from 1 to 8 miles, providing a variety of half day hikes, more or less, depending upon your fitness level. Several trails can also be combined for a longer hike.

We hope you experience as much enjoyment from using this guidebook as we did from creating it!

Robert & Jenny Fuller
halfdayhikes.com

Acknowledgements

This book is Half Day Hikes' way of sharing our passion for hiking and love for the great outdoors.

We would like to take this opportunity to thank several key employees at Texas Parks & Wildlife who, without their support and assistance, this book would have not been possible:

Rodney Franklin
Director
Texas Parks & Wildlife

Kevin Good
Special Assistant to the Director
Texas Parks & Wildlife

Nathanael Gold
Superintendent, Big Bend Ranch State Park Complex
Big Bend Ranch State Park

Amber Harrison
Park Ranger-Interpreter
Barton Warnock Visitor Center
Big Bend Ranch State Park

Kirsten Corda
Texas Master Naturalist
Assistant Office Manager & Visitor Services
Sauceda Ranger Station
Big Bend Ranch State Park

A special thank you to all the wonderful staff and volunteers at Big Bend Ranch State Park who make the park available to visitors each and every day.

Contents

*Note:

Plan ahead. Allow for at least a 90 minute drive on the dirt road from FM 170 to reach the Sauceda Ranger Station. Refer to the Introduction, Vehicle Awareness, and Safety Tips for planning essentials.

Botella Junction – Internal Park Entrance (unattended)

Introduction
Big Bend Ranch State Park

Big Bend Ranch State Park is the largest state park in Texas. The 300,000 acres of desert landscape offer some of the most rugged and remote public land in Texas.

For the adventurer seeking solitude and a backcountry experience, there are 238 miles of multi-use trails open to hikers, mountain bikers, and equestrians. This includes 70 miles of unmaintained dirt roads for high-clearance and four-wheel-drive vehicles to explore.

Big Bend Ranch State Park provides a fantastic opportunity to experience the Chihuahuan Desert's wildlife, plants, geology, and stunning vistas of the surrounding mountains. It's also designated as an International Dark Sky Park, offering excellent stargazing opportunities.

There are two main access points into the park: the east entrance at the Barton Warnock Visitor Center, one mile east of Lajitas on FM 170 (also known as Camino Del Rio/ River Road); and the west entrance at the Fort Leaton Historic Site, four miles southeast of Presidio, also on FM 170.

The Sauceda Ranger Station is the interior outpost of Big Bend Ranch State Park and is ONLY accessible by a 27-mile rugged dirt road from FM 170. This road is the only way in and out of the interior of the park. Due to road conditions and many tight blind corners, motor homes and travel trailers are not recommended. The speed limit is 25 mph; expect to take approximately 90 minutes to drive to the Sauceda Ranger Station from FM 170, depending on weather and road conditions.

The interior of Big Bend Ranch State Park is very remote with limited services; cell phone service is almost non-existent. The trip is well worth the adventure and solitude if you have the appropriate vehicle, plan ahead, and follow the tips below. We also recommend purchasing the Big Bend Ranch State Park Exploration Map, available at the parks' ranger station as a guide to carry with you at all times.

If you intend to spend multiple days in the interior of the park, we recommend reserving a campsite or hunkering down at the Sauceda Lodge Bunkhouse. For additional details, visit the Texas Parks & Wildlife website www.tpwd.texas.gov/bigbendranch or call the Sauceda Ranger Station, Barton Warnock Visitor Center, or Fort Leaton State Historic Site.

As required by all Texas State Parks, a permit is necessary for day use and camping (subject to availability). Permits can be purchased in person at the Sauceda Ranger Station, the Barton Warnock Visitor Center in Lajitas, or the Fort Leaton State Historic Site in Presidio.

Safety Tips

Visiting this remote park requires special attention to safety and an understanding of where you are. There is no hospital nearby and no helicopter on call, so help is, at best, four or more hours away, depending upon your location in the park and your ability to alert a Park Ranger. Add extreme temperatures and spotty cell phone service into the mix makes being prepared vital for your safety.

Emergency Preparedness

- **Don't hike alone**. If you do, tell someone your plans and estimated return time.

- Carry a first aid kit, extra food and water, a LifeStraw water filter, and high-energy snacks.

- Contact the nearest Park Ranger Station in an emergency situation. Program the Park Ranger Station numbers into your phone and keep a handwritten copy in your pack.

Sauceda Ranger Station:	(432) 358-4444
Barton Warnock Visitor Center:	(432) 424-3327
Fort Leaton State Historic Site:	(432) 229-3613

Communication

- Cell phone service is generally unavailable—do not rely on it!

- 911 service is many hours away IF you have signal.

- Be prepared to be self-sufficient in an emergency situation.

- Carry a GPS satellite communicator, if you have one.

Water

- Hydration is key to hiking in the desert.

- Carry and consume a minimum of one quart of water for each hour on the trail (one gallon per day, minimum) to avoid dehydration.

- Carrying additional water is recommended due to the remote location and heat.

Gear

- Carry a compass and the Big Bend Ranch State Park "Exploration Map" at all times.

- Use a GPS navigation device to track your hike. In the event you get lost, you can retrace your steps.

- Good hiking boots are essential in rough terrain. Do not hike in sneakers or sandals.

- Take a hiking pole to improve balance over rough terrain.

- Pack sunscreen and reapply frequently.

- Wear a cap or broad-brimmed hat.

Flash Flooding

- Flash flooding is prevalent in the area, especially in slot canyons and arroyos, which can quickly become raging torrents due to rainfall upstream. Never cross rain-swollen streams.

- Check with a Park Ranger for conditions if rain is expected or has recently fallen.

Weather

- **Temperature:** Can fluctuate by 30+ degrees in a day and is unpredictable. Refer to the weather table on Page 5 and plan accordingly.

- **Avoid the heat:** Desert heat is deadly. Apply sunscreen regularly, and avoid strenuous activity during the hottest part of the day.

- **Lightning storms**: Avoid elevated mountaintops and get to lower ground. Avoid lone tall trees and try to become the smallest target possible in an unexposed area. Discard metal hiking poles and keep away from wire fences.

Average Weather					
	Barton Warnock Visitors Center – FM 170/River Road Elevation: 2,403'			Sauceda Ranger Station – Park Interior Elevation: 4,140'		
Month	Min °F	Max °F	Rain (in)	Min °F	Max °F	Rain (in)
Jan	31	68	0.43	30	61	0.38
Feb	37	75	0.21	34	68	0.17
Mar	45	83	0.22	42	76	0.30
Apr	54	92	0.23	50	83	0.17
May	64	97	1.00	57	89	0.49
Jun	74	104	1.00	67	95	1.30
Jul	75	102	1.77	68	91	1.88
Aug	75	102	1.35	67	91	2.38
Sept	68	96	1.17	62	86	2.45
Oct	57	90	0.63	52	81	0.72
Nov	44	77	0.81	39	70	0.64
Dec	35	70	0.27	31	63	0.33

Average Weather (2010 – 2019) Courtesy of the National Weather Service

Wildlife

- **Snakes:** Avoid snakes and always tap rocks and objects before moving them. If you are bitten, remove constricting clothing and jewelery. Clean and wrap the wound and splint the extremity if possible. Limit movement and avoid elevating the injury. Contact a Park Ranger or seek medical attention immediately.

- **Never feed wild animals:** Observe them from a safe distance.

- **Mountain lions**: Do not run if encountered. Face the lion, make noise, and try to look as large as possible. Pick up small children. Back away slowly. If attacked, fight back. Report sightings to park staff immediately.

Ethics

- Be respectful of other trail users as well as the park's natural and cultural resources.

- Take out everything you take in. Carry a bag for refuse, and collect trash along the way. Leave a trail in better condition than you found it!

- Leave everything exactly as you find it. Plants, animals, artifacts, and archeological features are protected by law and should not be damaged, disturbed, or collected.

- Stay on designated trails.

- Follow trail etiquette; everyone yields to horses; bikes yield to hikers.

TRAIL COURTESY
YIELD TO

Vehicle Awareness for Visiting the Park Interior

Road Conditions

- Call or visit one of the Ranger Stations, as roads can be impacted by rain and run-off.

Vehicle Preparedness

- Gasoline is unavailable within the park; plan accordingly.

- Ensure your vehicle is in excellent condition AND appropriate for the terrain.

- Carry at least one full-size spare tire in excellent condition AND the necessary equipment to change a tire.

- Be willing and able to change a tire without assistance.

Flatirons of the Solitario

Vehicle Accessibility and Road Recommendations

- **Graded (2WD):** A graded, unpaved road passable by standard vehicles when driven responsibly.

- **2-Wheel Drive High Clearance (2WDHC):** Unpaved road normally passable by standard street vehicles with high clearance.

- **4-Wheel Drive:** Primitive roads irregularly maintained requiring extra traction to accommodate steep grades, loose surfaces. Multiple spare tires advisable.

- **4-Wheel Drive High Clearance (4WDHC):** Primitive roads, harsher than 4WD—for the adventurer who is prepared to potentially build roads along the way. Must have 4WD with high clearance and multiple spare tires.

About this Guide

This book is designed as a "trail buddy" to help you plan your hiking adventure and to carry with you on the trail. Whether it's an early morning start to beat the heat and enjoy the perfect light as the sun rises, or a late afternoon hike to capture a stunning sunset at the end of the day, nature beckons, and our trail buddy is here to help you make the most of your hikes.

All trails are rated easy to moderate in complexity, ranging from 1 to 8 miles in distance, and can be completed in a half day, more or less. Several trails can also be combined.

For easy reference, the hikes are separated into two sections: trails accessible via the paved highway FM 170 (Camino Del Rio/River Road), and trails accessible via the interior unpaved Main Park Road, leading to the Sauceda Ranger Station and beyond. Each trail description has several sections to make planning and access easy, such as:

Trail Highlights

A brief overview to help you select a trail. Details on what to expect along the trail, including distance, difficulty, trail surface, trail usage, estimated hiking time, and photos of the hike's main features.

Trail Map and Reference Points

Trail map and key reference points to keep you on the right path.

INTERESTING FACT

Fun fact or history related to the hike.

How to Find the Trailhead

Driving and parking directions to the trailhead.

Trail Reference Guide

On the next page, you will find a list of all hikes described in this guidebook outlining trail distance, trail type, difficulty, estimated hiking time, and if the trail is dog friendly.

What It's Not

Half Day Hikes is all about "the hike"—we are not natural history or geology experts. Our goal is simple: to provide trail insights to make the most of your time on the trail.

Information regarding the history, geology, wildlife, flora, and fauna of Big Bend Ranch State Park is readily available from the Texas Parks & Wildlife's Park Ranger Stations and on the Internet to complement our trail buddy. Our research has shown that this information is rarely accessed on the trail, so in most cases these books are best referenced before and after your hike, and not weighing down your pack.

Trail Reference Guide

Hike	Trail Name	Miles	Dog Friendly	Highlights	Difficulty	Estimated Time	Page
Trails accessible from FM 170/River Road							
1	Hoodoos	1.1	√	Rio Grande views, rock formations	Easy	45 mins.	11
2	Closed Canyon	1.4	√	Slot canyon, bird life	Easy/Moderate	< 1 hour	15
3	Rancherias Canyon	6.0 to 8.0	×	Riparian area, birds, geology	Moderate	4.0 – 6.0 hours	20
4	Contrabando Trail - East	7.2	×	Historic wax camp, crystals	Easy	3.0 – 3.5 hours	26
5	Fresno Divide	7.0 or 8.3	×	Flatiron views, mine ruins	Moderate	3.5 – 4.5 or 5.0 – 6.0	33
Trails accessible from Big Bend Ranch State Park Interior							
6	Sauceda Nature Trail	0.9	×	Great sunset hike, desert plants	Easy	30 mins.	42
7	Horsetrap	5.0	×	Desert landscape	Easy	2.0 hours	46
8	Ojito Adentro	1.4	×	Birdlife, springs, native ferns	Easy	< 1 hour	51
9	Papalote Rancho Viejo	1.0	×	Corral and Homestead ruins	Easy	45 mins.	55
10	West Fresno Rim	5.0	×	Flatiron views, cacti variety	Easy/Moderate	2.5 hours	59
11	Cerro Chilicote Loop	3.2	×	Desert landscape	Easy	1.5 hours	64
12 A or 12 B	Cinco Tinajas	1.0 or 3.0	×	Rock art, pour-off, scenic view, tinajas	Easy/Moderate	45 mins. - 2.0 hours	69

12/30/19   1.87mi

Hoodoos

Trail Highlights

An easy loop trail with unique geological rock formations known as "Hoodoos," with stunning views of the Rio Grande.

The Hoodoos are easily accessible and can be seen from the parking area trailhead.

Approximate Distance:	1.1-mile loop trail
Difficulty:	Easy
Trail Surface:	Mix of rock and dirt, with a moderate change of slope
Estimated Time:	45 minutes
Trail Usage:	Hiking

CAUTION: Exercise extreme caution if it has been raining in the region, as rainfall far upstream can result in flash flooding!

The Hike and Trail

Start from the parking area and follow the clearly marked trailhead sign down to the trail sign identifying the intersection of the trail leading to the overlook and the trail down toward the Hoodoos. Hike clockwise up the short hill to the overlook for a great view of the Hoodoos with the Rio Grande in the background.

Continue on the spur trail to the southeast (left) of the lookout for an impressive view of the Rio Grande River winding to the south. Follow the rock cairns, rock baskets, and trail arrows down toward the riverbank. The trail turns northwest (right) and follows the Rio Grande along a sandy path for about half a mile before heading toward the Hoodoos on your right. Note: If it has been raining the trail may be difficult to find. Follow the river until you see another rock basket trail marker on your right.

The Rio Grande from the scenic overlook

Continue along the trail to the Hoodoos for a perfect photo opportunity with the Rio Grande as a backdrop. Continue following the rock markers to complete the loop, and then hike back up to the parking area.

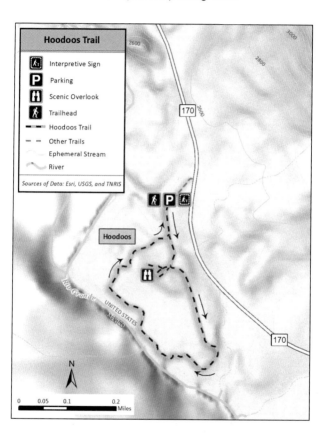

Approximate Distance	Reference Points
225 yards	Parking area to overlook
1.1 miles	Entire loop trail

- If you have limited time, we recommend going directly to the overlook and taking the short, steep trail down to the Hoodoos.

- If you hike the entire loop, we recommend a clockwise direction. Visit the overlook then follow the trail down to the Rio Grande and over to the Hoodoos for the best views.

- The trail is a little difficult to follow by the river. Look for trail arrows, rock cairns, and rock basket trail markers and follow the river bank.

- This is one of two trails in Big Bend Ranch State Park that allow dogs on a leash. Bring your four-legged friends, but please clean up after them.

- To help preserve the Hoodoos, do not climb on them or disturb the nearby rocks.

- There is a self-pay station located in the parking area if you need to purchase a state park permit.

INTERESTING FACT

Hoodoos are also known as Tent Rocks, Goblins, and Fairy Chimneys due to their interesting shapes. They are mainly found in the desert.

These Hoodoos have been formed by millions of years of erosion by wind and rain, as the lower column is made of tuff, a softer, more erodible material.

Finding the Trailhead

The Hoodoos trailhead is located approximately 26 miles west of the Barton Warnock Visitor Center and 22 miles east of Fort Leaton State Historic Site on FM 170 (Camino Del Rio/River Road).

Trail 2: Closed Canyon

12/30/19   1.4mi

Closed Canyon

Trail Highlights

An impressive hike through a narrow slot canyon that divides Colorado Mesa in two: Mesa de la Cuchilla to the east, and Mesa de Nueve to the west. The undefined trail winds through the tall canyon walls leading toward the Rio Grande River.

Views of the Rio Grande and access to the river is not possible without rappelling equipment and mountaineering experience, and is therefore not recommended.

Approximate Distance:	1.4 mile out and back
Difficulty:	Easy to moderate
Trail Surface:	Sand, gravel, rock, and pour-offs
Estimated Time:	Less than an hour
Trail Usage:	Hiking

The Hike and Trail

Begin the hike at the back of the parking area, to the right of the shelter. Hike down the short hill following the trail for just under a quarter of a mile, reaching the arroyo and entering the narrow walls of the canyon. Continue hiking through the winding canyon walls of the slot canyon, where you will reach several pour-offs requiring scrambling. The pour-offs become progressively steeper as you continue into the canyon. Some may require scrambling to reach the lower level. The rocks are very smooth with gravel bottoms and can be slick and slippery after rain. Carefully evaluate and navigate the slick rocks to avoid injury. Don't go down a pour-off if you think it will be a challenge to climb back up.

At 0.7 miles (or earlier, depending upon your comfort level) the hike ends, as the pour-offs now require rappelling and climbing gear. Use caution. This is an out and back hike, so you will return by retracing your steps back to where you entered the canyon and up to the parking area.

Closed Canyon

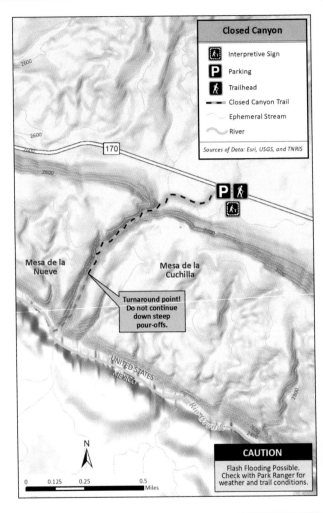

Approximate Distance	Reference Points
0.23 mile	Reach entrance to Closed Canyon
0.7 mile	End of trail; turn around
1.4 miles	Arrive back at trailhead parking area

Tips

- For most of the day Closed Canyon is typically in shade. Avoid hiking during midday when the sun is directly overhead.

- The canyon is home to a variety of birds and is a favorite habitat of the Canyon Wren.

- The trail is easy. However, hikers need to be able to maneuver up and down several pour-offs, so agility is necessary.

- River access is not intended on this hike and is only possible with vertical climbing equipment and mountaineering experience.

- There is a self-pay station located in the parking area if you need to purchase a state park permit.

- Dogs on a leash are allowed, but use caution as you reach the drop-offs, as they may not be able to get back out.

INTERESTING FACT

Colorado Mesa was created 28 million years ago from the deposition of welded tuff from the Santana and San Carlos calderas. A small stream was established in the tuff that eroded away to create the canyon. Millions of years of carving through the Santana Tuff divided the canyon into two, forming what we know as Closed Canyon.

Finding the Trailhead

The Closed Canyon Trailhead parking area is located approximately 22 miles west of the Barton Warnock Visitor Center and 26 miles east of Fort Leaton State Historic Site on FM 170 (Camino Del Rio/River Road). The trail starts at the back of the parking area, to the right of the shelter.

Trail 3: Rancherias Canyon

Hiking Rancherias Canyon Trail

Trail Highlights

A moderate out and back hike in the heart of the Bofecillos Mountains that gently climbs through the Chihuahuan Desert and passes through two distinctly different landscapes. Initially, the trail meanders through a barren desert landscape comprised of typical desert plants (ocotillo, prickly pear, and creosote bushes) and upon entering the dry wash of the Rancherias Canyon drainage, continues through a wonderful riparian area lush with native grasses, small cottonwood groves, and miniature colorful desert wildflowers (seasonal).

The Rancherias Canyon Trail is a delightful morning hike with a lot of variety, interesting geological rock formations, partial shade, and easy access from FM 170. Water is often present in the lower section of the canyon, attracting diverse wildlife.

Approximate Distance:	6.0 - 8.0* miles total - out and back
Difficulty:	Moderate
Trail Surface:	Gravel creek beds and a mix of small to large rocks and boulders
Estimated Time:	4.0 – 6.0 hours*
Trail Usage:	Hiking

* Distance and Time determined by turnaround point and fitness level.

> **CAUTION:** Flash flooding is possible in Rancherias Canyon. Call the Ranger Station for weather and trail conditions before entering the canyon.

The Hike and Trail

Follow the trail to the right of the parking area for just over half a mile as it gently climbs through the barren desert landscape, reaching a trail junction and the official Rancherias Canyon Trailhead sign.

Continue to the right, following the **Rancherias Canyon trail** down the hill until you reach the floor of the canyon. Veer left following the rock cairns up the dry creek bed. There is a significant change in vegetation due to the presence of water from the spring.

Continue along the creek bed for a short distance, following the rock cairns leading to the right and up a short rock scramble before the trail veers left and continues up the canyon.

The trail climbs gently, and the terrain is mainly sand and gravel with a mix of small to large rocks and boulders. Be careful and watch where you walk, as it would be easy to twist an ankle due to unstable rocks. In just under 2 miles, you will reach a large rock overhang on the right, providing a great shaded spot for a quick break from the sun and to take in the surrounding peace and tranquility.

At the end of the rock overhang, the trail veers to the left (northwest) toward an impressive large red rock face in the distance. As you continue up the canyon, you will pass by a series of underground springs identified by a small grove of cottonwood and willow trees. Just after the grove there is a great example of a conglomerate rock on your left. As you approach the canyon wall, the trail now veers to the right. The high canyon walls formed by the Bofecillos and Sierra Rica volcanoes now begin to narrow and snake through the canyon with several species of small, colorful, native wildflowers growing along the canyon floor.

Continuing up the canyon the vegetation becomes thicker, passing through several areas with river cane, long native grasses, and dense vegetation. If you reach 4.0 miles the canyon widens and provides stunning views back down the canyon toward Mexico.

On this trail, we recommend turning around after hiking for two hours. It is not recommended to hike beyond

Rancherias Canyon - Northern View

4.0 miles as the vegetation becomes very thick and continuing will extend your overall hiking time considerably.

From your turnaround point, retrace your steps back through the canyon, carefully following the rock cairns and enjoying the scenery, birdlife, and vegetation on the return trip.

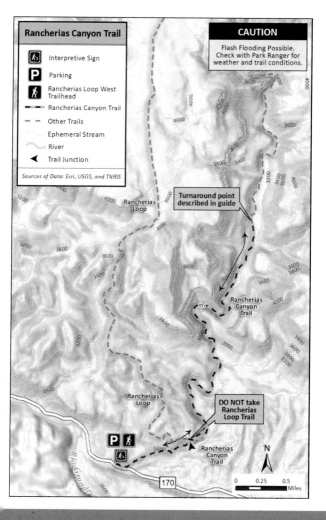

Approximate Distance	Reference Points
0.6 mile	Reach trailhead sign for Rancherias Loop and Rancherias Canyon. Turn right, following Rancherias Canyon trail down toward the canyon floor.
1.0 mile	Reach canyon floor. Turn left, following the rock cairns up the dry creek bed.
1.98 miles	Approach a rock overhang on your right with shade. Trail veers left (northwest).
	Continue hiking on the trail for up to 2 hours. Turnaround and return along the same trail, retracing your steps back to the parking area.
4.0 miles**	The canyon opens up, providing excellent views up and down the canyon. Turnaround point.
5.98 miles	Reach rock overhang, now on your left. Turn right and retrace your steps.
7.0 miles	Look for the rock cairn on the right, identifying the trail that climbs back up to the main trailhead intersection. Turn right.
7.25 miles	Reach trail junction of Rancherias Loop and Rancherias Canyon. Turn left (south).
8.0 miles	Arrive at parking area.

**Maximum distance recommended

Tips

■ As this is an **out and back** hike, you can turn around at any point.

■ Track time on this hike, over distance — 2 hours out (for a total of 4 hours) for a half day hike.

■ The official state park trail continues to Rancherias Falls. Our recommendation is to hike a **maximum** of 4.0 miles out and turn around. Beyond this point the trail becomes difficult to navigate with dense vegetation and makes for a very long hike.

■ The hike becomes more scenic after the first mile, after you reach the canyon floor. Hike in the morning to take advantage of the shade provided by the canyon walls.

- Use a hiking pole for stability on the rocky terrain.

- Wear hiking boots with ankle support due to unstable rocks.

- Try to avoid walking on wildflowers and new growth on the canyon floor.

Rancherias Canyon lies within the Bofecillos Mountains and was formed 27 million years ago from extensive lava flows and volcanic ash.

Finding the Trailhead

The Rancherias Canyon and Rancherias Loop Trailhead is located on Highway FM 170, approximately 23 miles west of Barton Warnock Ranger Station and approximately 27 miles east of the Fort Leaton State Historic Site.

Rancherias Canyon view

Trail 4: Contrabando Trail – East Trailhead
Dog Cholla, Crystal, Rock Quarry & Buena Suerte Trails

View from Rock Quarry Trail

Trail Highlights

This easy half day hike on the Contrabando Multi-use Trail System (East Trailhead) links a combination of wagon paths (dating back to the early 1890s) with single-track hike and bike trails, for approximately 7 miles. On this loop trail you'll see plenty of desert fauna, historic ruins, and views of the North Lajitas Mesa and Contrabando Mountain.

Dog Cholla – a simple single-track trail named after the Cholla cacti you'll see along the trail.

Crystal – a single-track trail crossing several arroyos (dry creek beds) to a hilltop covered in pieces of quartz that shimmer in the desert sun.

Rock Quarry – a single-track trail winding through the low desert scrub with views of the Chisos Mountains in the distance.

Buena Suerte – an old wagon path intersecting each trail and passing by the historic ruins of a Candelilla wax camp. Also known as East Main Trail.

Approximate Distance:	7.2 miles round trip
Difficulty:	Easy
Trail Surface:	Dirt, sand, and gravel
Estimated Time:	3.0 – 3.5 hours
Trail Usage:	Hiking, Biking, Equestrian

The Hike and Trail

The vast and rugged landscape of the Chihuahua Desert is inspiring on this multi-use trail for hikers, bikers, and equestrians.

Start the hike on the **Dog Cholla Trail**, located through an opening in the fence on the left-hand side of the parking area. The single-track trail is fairly flat for half a mile and then undulates, passing through a mesquite grove with tall native grasses and abundant bird life. The trail continues through a barren section with lava rock, ocotillo, cholla cactus, creosote bushes, and low desert scrub with views of the North Lajitas Mesa to the west. In approximately 1 mile, after crossing a short wooden walkway, you'll reach the **Buena Suerte Trail**, an old wagon path. Turn left (north).

The Buena Suerte Trail is wider, and the vegetation consists mainly of creosote bushes and Candelilla plants until reaching the ruins of a Candelilla wax camp, which dates back to the 1940s. Candelilla plants are a common sight on this part of the trail, so it's easy to understand why the camp was established here.

We recommend reading the "Of Wax and Men" interpretive display located on the right-hand side of the trail to learn more about the history of the Candelilla wax camp. The actual wax camp ruins are located to the northeast across the wash on the far side. From the wax camp, continue along the Buena Suerte Trail for approximately a quarter of a mile. At the Crystal Trail junction, turn right (north) and continue along the **Crystal Trail**.

The trail weaves through the desert landscape, crossing several washes before reaching a hillside covered with quartz rocks glistening in the sun. Continue up and over the small, quartz-covered hill, heading west where the trail reconnects back to the Buena Suerte Trail.

Quartz hill on the Crystal Trail

At the intersection of Buena Suerte Trail and Crystal Trail, we begin the return journey. Turn left (southeast) back onto the **Buena Suerte Trail,** hiking for 0.61 of a mile before reaching the Rock Quarry Trailhead on your right. Turn right (southwest) onto the **Rock Quarry Trail**.

Follow the Rock Quarry Trail enjoying distant views of the Chisos Mountains to the east before reconnecting again with the Buena Suerte Trail in a mile. From here, hikers can enjoy views of the surrounding mountains and harsh desert landscape dotted with cacti, agave plants, and small wildlife critters.

At the junction of Rock Quarry Trail and Buena Suerte Trail, turn right (southeast) and continue hiking along the **Buena Suerte Trail**, passing by the Crystal Trailhead and Candelilla Wax Camp, visited on the way out. After just over a mile, you'll reach the Dog Cholla Trailhead sign. Turn right onto the **Dog Cholla Trail,** heading back to the parking area. [*Alternatively*, continue straight on the **Buena Suerte Trail,** which will also lead you back to the parking area.] Both trails are similar distances and end at the trailhead parking area.

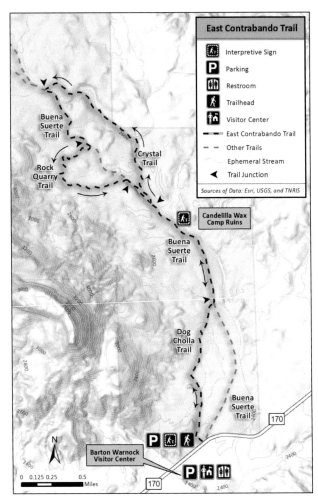

Note: Buena Suerte Trail is also known as East Main Trail

Contrabando Trail - East view

Tips

- The Contrabando Multi-use Trail System is composed of 25 miles of interconnecting trails. We selected four trails to make a loop trail that is easily accessible from the East Trailhead, just outside of Lajitas.

- The trail is very exposed and lacks shade; bring lots of sunscreen, water, and a hat.

- This is an easy introductory trail that's perfect for becoming familiar with the flora, fauna, geography, and hiking conditions in the area.

- To shorten the distance, return to the Buena Suerte Trail and hike south back to the trailhead and parking area.

- This trail is heavily used by mountain bikers, so keep an eye out for bikers while hiking.

- If you have a mountain bike, consider riding the single-track trails. Most of the trails are easy, with a few moderate rocky sections to navigate.

Approximate Distance	Reference Points
1.1 miles	Parking area trailhead to end of Dog Cholla. Turn left (north) onto Buena Suerte Trail.
1.7 miles	Reach the Candelilla wax camp.
2.0 miles	The intersection of Crystal and Buena Suerte Trails. Turn right (north) onto the Crystal Trail.
3.27 miles	Reach the quartz-covered hill.
3.4 miles	End of Crystal Trail. Turn left (southeast) on Buena Suerte Trail.
4.0 miles	Reach Rock Quarry Trail. Turn right (southwest).
5.0 miles	End of Rock Quarry Trail. Turn right (southeast) onto Buena Suerte Trail.
6.1 miles	Reach Dog Cholla Trail on right. Take either trail back to the trailhead.
7.2 miles	Reach trailhead and parking area.

INTERESTING FACTS

Ruins of a candelilla wax camp can be seen along the trail.

Candelilla wax processing peaked during World War I, when the U.S. Army used it to waterproof canvas, military tents, and ammunition.

The stems of the candelilla plant can also be harvested and used to make candles. Today, Candelilla is found in lip balm, crayons, and chewing gum.

Candelilla means "little candle" in Spanish.

Finding the Trailhead

The Contrabando East Trailhead parking is located a few hundred yards east of the Barton Warnock Visitor Center on FM 170, just outside the town of Lajitas.

12/31/19
7.27 mi 4hr

Scenic Overlook and Contrabando Dome

Trail Highlights

An easy to moderate 7.0 mile out and back hike on the Contrabando Multi-use Trail System, starting from the Contrabando West Trailhead.

Trail highlights include excellent views of the Bofecillos Mountains, Fresno Creek, the Contrabando Dome, and the Flatirons of the Solitario.

Approximate Distance:	7.0 mile out and back
Difficulty:	Moderate
Trail Surface:	Dirt and sand
Estimated Time:	3.5 – 4.5 hours
Trail Usage:	Hiking, Biking, Equestrian

Fresno Divide Trail View

The Hike and Trail

From the Contrabando West Trail System parking area follow the road down the hill, past the campsite (on the right) and through the wooden vehicle barrier on the right. Hike downhill, passing by rustic mining equipment at the bottom of the hill on your left. Continue along the dirt road until you reach the wooden trailhead signs indicating the intersection of the Contrabando and West Contrabando trails. Follow the **Contrabando Trail** through another set of wooden bollards, reaching a metal trail sign at the intersection of the Fresno Divide Trail and the West Main Trail in just over 0.3 of a mile.

Turn left (north) onto the **Fresno Divide Trail**, following the rock cairns and rock alignments along a well-worn single-track trail that passes through native scrub.

In just under 1.5 miles, the trail climbs slightly to a low terrace providing a panoramic view of the Fresno Creek (which is likely dry, except after recent rain) on the left, where the creek passes through a gully close to the trail. In a short distance, the trail heads south and meanders down and around several small hills, then gently traverses uphill over red volcanic rock. The rock formations along the trail were formed millions of years ago and provide many textures and layers. In just over 2 miles from the trailhead, the Flatirons of the Solitario can be seen in the distance together with the Bofecillos Mountains.

After hiking approximately 3.5 miles, you'll reach a scenic lookout with a great view of the Flatirons of the Solitario to the left (north) and the Contrabando Dome (southeast). The level of volcanic activity that can be seen from this vantage point is impressive. This is the turnaround point for the out and back hike. *[Alternatively, for a longer hike refer to Pages 38-41 to return via Dome & West Main Trails.]*

After enjoying the views, retrace your steps back along the **Fresno Divide Trail**, following the rock cairns and rock alignments to the Fresno Creek scenic overlook. Continue along the trail to the intersection of **Fresno Divide Trail** and **West Main Trails** where you originally joined the **Fresno Divide Trail**. Turn right, passing through the wooden bollards and continue along and up the dirt road. Pass through the wooden vehicle barrier and turn left, walking by the campsite on your left and up the hill to return to your vehicle.

INTERESTING FACT

The mineral cinnabar was mined in this area in the 1940s to extract mercury. Cinnabar was also known as "quicksilver" due to its fluidity. To extract the mercury, the cinnabar was heated in large furnaces to free entrapped quicksilver through evaporation. After cooling and condensing the quicksilver on-site, it was shipped to market in lead flasks.

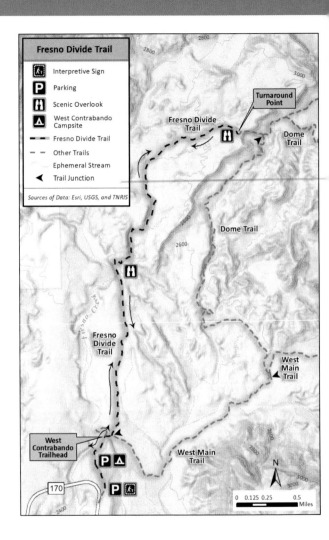

Fresno Divide Trail

- 🚶 Interpretive Sign
- 🅿 Parking
- 🚻 Scenic Overlook
- 🔺 West Contrabando Campsite
- ▬▬ Fresno Divide Trail
- – – Other Trails
- Ephemeral Stream
- ◄ Trail Junction

Sources of Data: Esri, USGS, and TNRIS

Turnaround Point

Fresno Divide Trail

Dome Trail

Dome Trail

Fresno Divide Trail

Fresno Creek

West Main Trail

West Contrabando Trailhead

West Main Trail

170

N

0 0.125 0.25   0.5
                    Miles

Approximate Distance	Reference Points
0.17 miles	Parking area to rustic mining equipment on the left-hand side of the road.
0.2 miles	Reach the intersection of Contrabando and West Contrabando trails. Continue right on the West Contrabando Trail.
0.3 miles	Reach the Fresno Divide and West Main Trail intersection (metal sign). Turn left onto Fresno Divide Trail.
1.5 miles	View of the seasonal Fresno Creek below, to the left.
3.5 miles	Reach overlook with views of the Flatirons of the Solitario to the west. Turnaround point for out and back hike.
5.5 miles	Pass scenic overlook of the Fresno Creek on return trip.
6.7 miles	Reach Fresno Divide Trailhead.
7.0 miles	Return to parking area.

Finding the Trailhead

The hike begins at the West Contrabando Trail System parking area, 6.5 miles west of the Barton Warnock Visitor Center on FM 170 (Camino Del Rio/River Road) and approximately 42 miles east of Fort Leaton State Historic Site. Park at the first designated parking area (on your left) after exiting FM 170, where the interpretive sign and trail map is located.

To find the trailhead, follow directions under "The Hike and Trail" on Page 34.

OPTIONAL Return Trail for Fresno Divide/Hike #5

Extended hike returning via Dome & West Main Trails to create a Loop Trail increasing the overall hiking distance to 8.3 miles and hiking time up to 6 hours in duration.

This return hike begins at the Scenic Overlook (at the intersection of the orange and blue trails highlighted on the map on Page 40) and provides the opportunity to visit two small ruins of former cinnabar (mercury) mines, dating back to the 1940s, and interesting rock formations created by volcanic activity millions of years ago.

The Hike and Trail *[Continuing from the Scenic Overlook following the blue trail highlighted on the map.]*

After enjoying the views, continue on the trail, passing through the opening in the fence and down the short steep hill, reaching the junction of the Dome and Fresno Divide Trail at the bottom. Turn right (south) and follow the **Dome Trail** as it gently undulates downhill. The terrain becomes rocky with an abundance of Candelilla plants.

Ancient volcanic activity, followed by significant erosion has created interesting geological formations, canyons and arroyos that can be seen along this hike.

After hiking a total distance of approximately 4.7 miles, the remains of a former cinnabar mine and "Quicksilver" interpretive sign can be viewed, where mining for cinnabar occurred back in the 1940s. A small ruin of the miners' homes remains, reinforcing the harsh environment and isolation the miners dealt with while searching for "quicksilver," the mercury that was extracted from the cinnabar.

Continue following the trail downhill, passing the occasional metal trail arrow and rock cairn, into a creek bed for a short time before reaching the second mine camp and "Quicksilver" interpretive sign. This mine camp highlights the hardship endured by Homer Wilson and Harris Smith in their search for cinnabar back in the 1940s.

Continue hiking along the trail until you reach the intersection of the West Main Trail and Dome Trail after about 6.2 miles. Turn right onto the **West Main Trail** and follow the rock cairns in and out of several washes while enjoying the views of the surrounding mountains.

Continue following the West Main Trail signs until reaching the original intersection of the Fresno Divide Trail. Turn left passing through the wooden bollards and continue along and up the dirt road. Pass through the wooden vehicle barrier and turn left, walking by the campsite on your left and up the hill to return to your vehicle.

Approximate Distance	Reference Points from Fresno Divide Scenic Overlook
3.5 miles	Reach overlook with views of the Flatirons of the Solitario to the west. Continue straight (east).
3.6 miles	Dome Trail and Fresno Divide Trail intersection. Turn right (south).
4.7 miles	Cinnabar mine and first Quicksilver interpretive sign.
5.8 miles	Mine camp and second Quicksilver interpretive sign.
6.2 miles	West Main Trail and Dome Trail intersection. Turn right (south, southeast).
8.0 miles	Reach Fresno Divide Trailhead.
8.3 miles	Return to parking area.

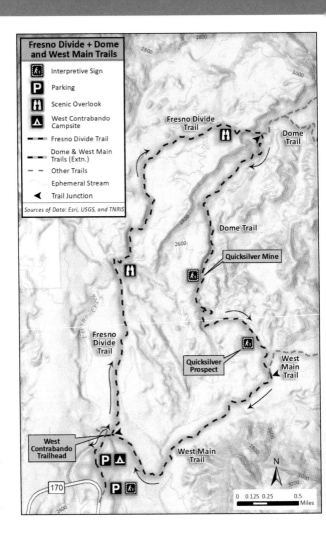

Tips

- No shade and very exposed; an early morning start is recommended.

- Very interesting geological area.

- This trail is commonly used by mountain bikers, so keep an eye out for bikers while hiking.

Fresno Divide Optional Return via Dome and West Main Trails

- Extending this trail makes for more than a half day hike; we strongly encourage hikers to evaluate pace, fitness and prepare for approximately 6 hours on the trail.

Dome Trail

Trail 6: Sauceda Nature Trail

Sunset at the trailhead

Trail Highlights

A short and easy loop trail to hike at sunset. Provides a lovely view from the hillside of the La Mota Mountain and the entire historic Sauceda complex. A display of native plants can be seen throughout the year along the trail with signs identifying the plant name. Depending upon the season and when you visit, the flowers may be in bloom.

Note: To create a loop trail, we include a short walk along the Main Park Road to return to the starting point.

Approximate Distance:	0.9 mile loop
Difficulty:	Easy
Trail Surface:	Sand and volcanic rock
Estimated Time:	30 minutes
Trail Usage:	Hikers

The Hike and Trail

The trailhead starts just past the fire ring to the right (west) of the Bunkhouse, initially weaving through a flat, sandy area with mostly creosote bushes and mesquite trees.

The trail traverses eastward up a small hill, passing by various examples of desert plants and succulents with signs identifying their names. Continue up the hill, walking on the lava rock and following the rock cairns until you reach the ridge. Here, the trail levels out and provides a bird's eye view over the entire Sauceda Historic Ranch complex and an excellent view of La Mota Mountain to the north.

Follow the rock cairns for a short distance to the north side of the ridge. The trail descends to the Main Park Road and trailhead, where you turn left and walk along the road, returning to the Sauceda Ranger Station.

Sauceda Ranch Complex

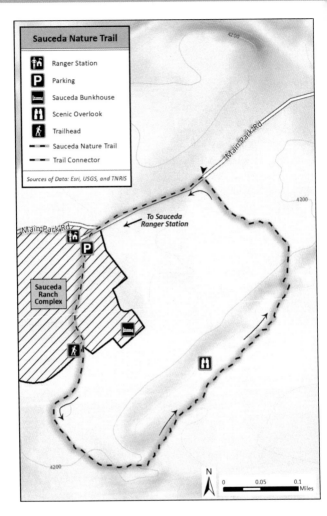

Approximate Distance	Reference Points
0.9 miles	Loop trail. Easy to follow.

- Walk the trail counter clockwise.

- Great sunset walk.

- Be mindful of rattlesnakes and javelina.

INTERESTING FACTS

The Chihuahuan Desert has 3,000 plant species, including more than 500 of the world's 1,500 species of cacti. The Nature Trail provides examples of several of the most common plants found in the area.

Finding the Trailhead

The trailhead is located across the driveway from the Sauceda Ranger Station, to the west of the Bunkhouse just past the fire ring. Look for the wooden "Nature Trail" sign.

Trail 7: Horsetrap

Horsetrap Trailhead

Trail Highlights

An easy 5.0-mile loop trail, including a 0.8-mile walk along Javelin Road and the Main Park Road to complete the loop.

Views include the most prominent La Mota Mountains to the north and the majestic Fresno Peak. On a clear day you may be able to see the Flatirons of the Solitario in the far distance, to the southeast. In the morning, you'll likely have deer, longhorns, rabbits, and birds join you on the trail.

The trail is situated at the junction of the Llano Pasture and the foothills of the Bofecillos Mountains. "Llano" is Spanish for plain and describes a landscape with desert grassland, low hills, and rocky outcrops—providing a perfect description of what to expect on this trail.

Approximate Distance:	5.0 mile loop
Difficulty:	Easy
Trail Surface:	Rocky and sandy
Estimated Time:	2.0 hours
Trail Usage:	Hiking, Biking, Equestrian

The Hike and Trail

This hike can be done in both directions. We recommend hiking the trail counterclockwise, starting from the Horsetrap Trailhead on the Main Park Road, just down from the Sauceda Ranger Station.

Follow the well-defined trail through creosote bushes, sotol plants, and low desert scrub. Distant views of an old corral on your right are evidence of ranching activities dating back to the early 1900s.

Following the rock cairns, the trail gently ascends up a small hill, providing a great view over the Historic Sauceda Ranch Complex to the east and views of the surrounding mountains. In approximately 2.0 miles, the trail passes through an open barbed wire fence and loops back toward the Sauceda Ranch Complex.

The trail flattens out, and after crossing several washes, the cottonwood trees at Horsetrap Springs can be seen in the distance. Continue along the trail toward Horsetrap Springs, located just before the Javelin Road trailhead. The springs are mainly underground but easily identified by the lush cottonwood trees. At the trailhead, turn left and head north on Javelin Road, and continue for 0.6 miles, passing by staff housing, horse stables, and the ranch service yard.

Horsetrap Trail View

Turn left on the Main Park Service Road, and continue for 0.2 miles to arrive back at the Horsetrap Trailhead and parking area.

Tips

- The trail can be hiked in either direction.
- Easy hike directly accessible from Sauceda Ranger Station.
- Excellent morning hike or trail-run workout.
- Exposed trail with zero shade. If the sun is very strong, hike the trail counterclockwise so the sun is behind you.
- Watch for mountain bikers.

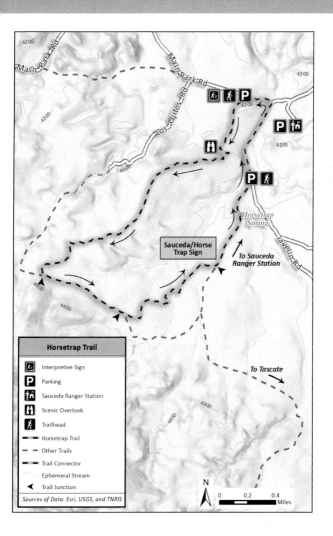

Horsetrap Trail

🏞	Interpretive Sign
🅿	Parking
🏠	Sauceda Ranger Station
🍴	Scenic Overlook
🚶	Trailhead
▬▬▬	Horsetrap Trail
▬ ▬	Other Trails
▬▬▬	Trail Connector
▬▬▬	Ephemeral Stream
◀	Trail Junction

Sources of Data: Esri, USGS, and TNRIS

Sauceda/Horse Trap Sign

To Sauceda Ranger Station

To Tascate

Horsetrap Spring

N

0   0.2   0.4
Miles

Approximate Distance	Reference Points:
0.4 miles	Reach a lookout over Sauceda complex.
2.0 miles	Hike through an open barbed wire fence.
3.5 miles	Reach the Sauceda and Horsetrap metal trail sign at a trail junction.
4.0 miles	Horsetrap Springs identified by the cottonwood trees.
4.1 miles	Arrive at Horsetrap Trailhead on Javelin Road; turn left, heading toward Sauceda Ranger Station.
4.7 miles	Reach Main Park Road. Turn left.
5.0 miles	Return to parking area.

INTERESTING FACTS

Sauceda Ranch was established around 1905 and had a long history of goat, sheep, and cattle ranching until 1988, when the property was designated as a state park.

Remains of an old corral can be seen from the western segment of the trail, near the trailhead. These corrals were used for rodeos from around 1950–1970 to entertain the families living at the ranch.

Finding the Trailhead

To hike the trail counterclockwise, the trailhead is approximately 0.2 miles west of the Sauceda Ranger Station on the left-hand side of the Main Park Road. The parking area is located across the road on the right.

Alternatively, to hike the trail clockwise, walk or drive, 0.6 mile down Javelin Road—the first road on the left as you leave the Ranger Station—to the alternate trailhead, which will be on your right.

Trail 8: Ojito Adentro

Ojito Adentro waterfall/seep

Trail Highlights

A short, easy to moderate hike to Ojito Adentro, which translates to "a small spring" in Spanish. The Ojito Adentro Trail is located within the Bofecillos Mountains, just below Agua Adentro Mountain. The trail leads to several springs with shade provided by the cottonwood trees and the Ojito Adentro waterfall (a seep with a trickle of water) where native grapevines and maidenhair ferns thrive most of the year. A true riparian zone, and one of the best birding places within the park.

Note: A short portion (less than 100 yards) of the trail requires scrambling over large boulders to reach the seasonal waterfall/seep with the native vines and ferns.

Approximate Distance:	1.4 mile out and back
Difficulty:	Easy with a 100-yard moderate rock scramble
Trail Surface:	Rocks and sand
Estimated Time:	0.75 – 1 hour
Trail Usage:	Hiking

The Hike and Trail

Follow the trail marked by rock cairns and begin the hike down the undulating rocky trail, toward the cottonwood trees in the distance. After half of a mile, the trail reaches the Ojito Adentro Springs, shaded by cottonwood trees and full of active bird life.

After a short distance and a scramble over several large boulders and tree branches (approximately 100 yards), the trail ends at the seasonal waterfall/seep surrounded by lush native grapevines, willow trees, and maidenhair ferns. An impressive site considering you are in the desert!

Retrace your steps along the trail with a slight ascent back toward the parking area where you began your hike.

Tips

- Great walk to break up the drive to or from the Sauceda Ranger Station, located in the interior of the park.

- The boulder scramble requires agility and shoes with a good grip; use personal judgment before proceeding.

- The trail could be dense with vegetation, or muddy after heavy rains.

- One of the best birding location in the park—bring a camera and binoculars.

- Keep an eye out for poison oak.

- Depending on the season, there may be a lot of bee activity in the trees—proceed cautiously.

- The springs are sensitive habitats for many species of plants and animals, so please stay out of the water.

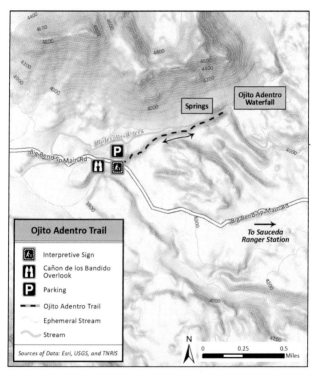

Approximate Distance	Reference Points
0.5 miles	Reach the beginning of the Ojito Adentro Springs and cottonwood grove; veer right.
0.6 miles	Beginning of rock scramble.
0.7 miles	Arrive at Ojito Adentro waterfall/seep and the trail end. Retrace your steps.
1.4 miles	Reach parking area.

Ojito Adentro Trail

Ojito Adentro is considered a **riparian zone**.

A riparian zone is an ecosystem that lies between the land and water, where water-dependent plants and animals live.

In Big Bend Ranch, riparian zones are typically small, isolated areas that occur along intermittent streams and springs.

Finding the Trailhead

The Ojito Adentro Trailhead is located 8.5 miles east of Botella Junction (the unattended park entrance) on the Main Park Road in the park's interior.

Trail 9: Papalote Rancho Viejo Ruins

Papalote Rancho Viejo Corral

Trail Highlights

An undefined trail starting near the Papalote Rancho Viejo campsite to a large stone corral in excellent condition, built meticulously of stone in the 1930s. Optionally, the ruins of an old ranch house can also be visited.

Note: This trail option DOES NOT follow the official 14.4-mile Rancho Viejo Trail that circumnavigates the Agua Adentro Mountains.

Approximate Distance:	1.0 mile out and back
Difficulty:	Easy, but no defined trail
Trail Surface:	Dirt and sand
Estimated Time:	45 minutes
Trail Usage:	Hiking

The Hike and Trail

From the parking area DO NOT take the official Rancho Viejo Trail; instead, walk along the road to the Papalote Rancho Viejo Campsite located next to the windmill and shelter. Please respect the privacy of campers and DO NOT cut through the campsite. Continue just past the campsite to an old water trough. Looking to the south, you will see the corral in the distance.

Head south toward the stone corral through an area where the creosote bushes are sparse. Halfway to the corral, cross a wash and continue to weave through another section of sparse creosote bushes until reaching the stone corral. On the far side of the corral there is a gate where you can enter the corral.

After viewing the corral, retrace your steps back to the wash. If you want to visit the old ranch house ruins, turn right and head up the wash toward the cottonwood trees in the distance. *[Otherwise, retrace your path back to the main road, using the windmill as a reference point.]*

Pass under the barbed wire strung across the wash and look for a large conglomerate boulder on the right-hand side of the wash with a rock cairn on top. Turn right before the cottonwood trees, and head out of the wash through the creosote bushes and small mesquite trees. If you reach the cottonwood trees, you have gone too far. From the wash, you cannot see the ranch house ruins, as it is hidden by dense vegetation.

After visiting the ranch house ruins, retrace your steps back to the wash and to the barbed wire strung across the wash. Turn right and follow the fence line up until you can see the windmill in the distance. Follow the trail in line with the windmill, leading you back towards the road, bypassing the campsite. Turn right and walk along the road to return to your vehicle.

Tips

- The road to the campsite is a 2WD road and does not require a 4WD vehicle.

- The stone corral is in very good condition; the ranch house is in poor condition (hence, it being optional).

- Bring a hiking pole to navigate through the creosote bushes on the way to the ranch house ruins.

- Don't stand on or disturb the corral or ranch house ruins.

- Respect the privacy of campers and do not walk through the campsite.

INTERESTING FACT

Mexican Vaqueros built Rancho Viejo's stone corral back in the 1930s. Its walls are approximately 6 feet thick and are in good condition.

Approximate Distance	Reference Points
250 yards	Walk back along the road past the campsite and windmill to the water trough. Turn left.
0.4 miles	Reach corral ruins.
0.56 miles	Return to the wash. Turn right, heading toward the cottonwood trees.
0.65 miles	Turn right at the boulder with the rock cairn on top; head toward the ranch house ruins.
1.0 miles	Return to the water trough and turn right and continue along the park road back to the parking area.

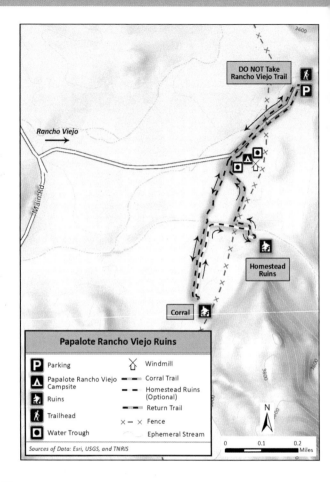

Finding the Trailhead

The trailhead turnoff is located approximately 3.5 miles from the park entrance on the Main Park Road. Park at the Ranch Viejo Trailhead, a short distance past the campsite. Walk back along the road, past the campsite to the water trough on your left to begin the hike.

Trail 10: West Fresno Rim

West Rim Overlook & Flatirons of the Solitario view

Trail Highlights

An easy to moderate out and back hike via Chilicote Springs, leading to a spectacular view of the Flatirons of the Solitario and a 700-foot cliff overlooking Fresno Canyon and Los Portales.

The trail leading to the West Fresno Rim overlook is very scenic with interesting volcanic rock formations and a wide variety of species of cacti and native desert plants.

Approximate Distance:	5.0 mile out and back
Difficulty:	Easy to moderate
Trail Surface:	Sand, rock, and dirt
Estimated Time:	2.5 hours
Trail Usage:	Hiking, Biking (allowed, but not recommended)

> **CAUTION:** Flash flooding is possible on some of the trails—especially in the washes. Check with the Park Ranger for weather and trail conditions.

The Hike and Trail

Begin at the second parking area and main trailhead. Follow the **Fresno Rim/Mexicano Falls trail** sign along the jeep trail for approximately 0.6 miles. Reaching the trail junction of West Fresno Rim Trail and Mexicano Falls Trail.

To visit the Chilicote Springs, follow the **Mexicano Falls trail** and rock cairns to the right, hiking over lava rock and boulders down into the wash, and toward the springs identified by the cottonwood trees.

After visiting the Chilicote Springs, retrace your steps back up the wash and to the West Fresno Rim Trail and Mexicano Trailhead sign. Turn right onto the **West Fresno Rim Trail**, and continue hiking for approximately 1.6 miles, carefully following the rock cairns while admiring the variety of desert vegetation, ancient volcanic activity, and surrounding vistas before reaching a short canyon descent.

Continue down the short, rocky trail, crossing the wash and following the trail along the base of the opposite canyon wall before ascending back up the canyon and reaching the West Fresno Rim Trail overlook in just under half a mile.

Enjoy the magnificent views of the Flatirons of the Solitario across Fresno Canyon, and Los Portales, just north of the Flatirons. Looking down into the canyon you can also see Fresno Creek, (which is likely dry, except after recent rain).

This is the perfect place to enjoy lunch or a snack before retracing your steps back to the trailhead and parking area.

West Fresno Rim Trail View

Approximate Distance	Reference Points
0.6 miles	Parking area to West Fresno Rim Trail/Mexicano Falls Trailhead junction.
	Arrive at Chilicote Springs in 200 feet.
	Return to the West Fresno Rim Trail/Mexicano Falls Trail junction. Follow the West Fresno Rim trail.
2.2 miles	Reach a short canyon descent; continue down the hill and across the wash and turn right, following the rock cairns.
2.5 miles	Reach the West Fresno Rim Canyon scenic overlook. Retrace your steps to the parking area, bypassing the Chilicote Springs.
5.0 miles	Reach the parking area and trailhead.

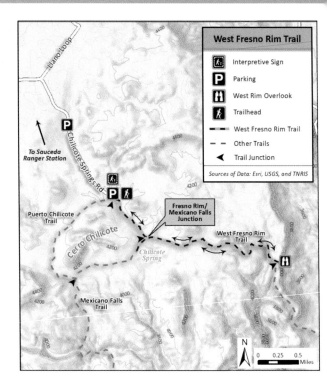

INTERESTING FACT

El Solitario is Spanish for "hermit" or "loner." It is the signature landscape feature of Big Bend Ranch State Park and is almost 10 miles across and almost symmetrical.

The Solitario was formed 36 million years ago and is a Laccolith with a caldera.

- The scenic overlook has an exceptional view of the Flatirons of the Solitario and is a great place to eat a snack and enjoy the view.

- Consider adding the Cerro Chilicote Loop for a longer hike. See page 64 for details.

- It can be very windy near the canyon rim/scenic overlook. It is not fenced off, so be cautious near the edge and pack a wind jacket.

- The road to the trailhead is suitable for 2-wheel drive vehicles, but you may need to park at the first parking area, depending on your vehicle's clearance.

Finding the Trailhead

From the Sauceda Ranger Station, drive east and pass the airstrip. Continue for approximately 1.7 miles, turn right onto the Llano Loop, then continue another 1.7 miles and turn left, following the Puerta Chilicote Trailhead signs.

Two parking areas are available; the first for vehicles that are unable to cross a small arroyo (one mile prior to the trailhead), and the second at the trailhead itself. The hike begins at the second trailhead.

Trail 11: Cerro Chilicote Loop

Cerro Chilicote Loop

Trail Highlights

An easy loop trail in the wild and rugged Bofecillos Highlands to the Chilicote Springs. The hike passes through several arroyos and provides interesting views of the Cerro Chilicote volcanic rock formations and old livestock fences, representative of the former ranching days in the area.

A great extension to Trail #10 - West Fresno Rim Trail, to make a longer hike.

Approximate Distance:	3.2 mile loop trail
Difficulty:	Easy
Trail Surface:	Dirt, sand, and volcanic rock
Estimated Time:	1.5 hours
Trail Usage:	Hiking, Biking (allowed, but not recommended)

> **CAUTION:** Flash flooding is possible on some of the trails—especially in the washes. Check with the Park Ranger for weather and trail conditions.

The Hike and Trail

Begin at the second parking area and main trailhead. Start hiking counterclockwise following the **Cerro Chilicote Loop** sign and rock cairns, initially passing by old livestock fences. Arrive at an underground spring with a cottonwood grove in a little over a mile.

Enter the wash on the left, following the rock cairns, and continue hiking along the wash for 0.4 of a mile; reach the Chilicote Springs Trailhead sign on the left.

Turn left, following the **Chilicote Trailhead** sign and carefully watch for rock cairns identifying the trail. Continue hiking along the trail for a little over a mile, passing by several species of cacti and enjoying the views of the interesting geological rock formations created by ancient volcanic activity. After a total of 2.6 miles from the trailhead, arrive at the Chilicote Springs, identified by a brilliant green cottonwood grove. A great place to take a break and enjoy the shade of the cottonwoods.

After a short break, follow the rock cairns up the wash to the left. The trail now veers right before reaching the Mexicano Falls and West Fresno Rim trails junction. At this junction, turn left and continue walking along the old jeep road for 0.6 miles to return to the parking area and complete the loop trail.

[*Alternatively*, to visit the West Fresno Rim scenic overlook, turn right onto on the West Fresno Rim Trail. Refer to Trail #10 – West Fresno Rim Trail and join the hike after visiting the Chilicote Springs on Page 60.]

Cerro Chilicote Trail

Approximate Distance	Reference Points
1.1 miles	Parking area to cottonwood grove and wash. Turn left.
1.5 miles	Reach the Chilicote Springs Trail sign. Turn left.
2.6 miles	Arrive at the Chilicote Springs.
2.7 miles	Reach the West Fresno Rim/Mexicano Falls trail intersection. Turn left.
3.2 miles	Arrive back at the trailhead parking area.

Tips

- Add the West Fresno Rim trail (an additional 3.8 mile hike) for a spectacular view of the Flatirons of the Solitario and Fresno Canyon.

- Take a break at Chilicote Springs and enjoy the shade of the cottonwood trees.

- Trail can be hiked in either direction.

- Watch for poison ivy at the Springs.

- The road to the trailhead is suitable for 2-wheel drive vehicles, but you may need to park at the first parking area, depending on your vehicle's clearance. Seek guidance from a Park Ranger.

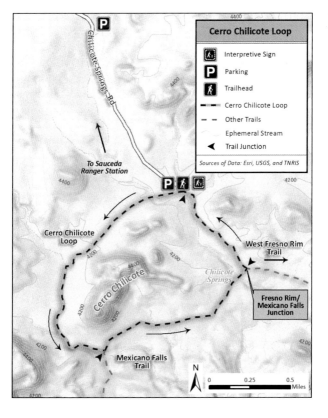

Cerro Chilicote is a remnant of Tertiary lava flows that occurred millions of years ago.

Finding the Trailhead

From the Sauceda Ranger Station drive east, passing by the airstrip, and continue for approximately 1.7 miles. Turn right onto the Llano Loop, then continue another 1.7 miles and turn left, following the Puerta Chilicote Trailhead signs.

Two parking areas are available; the first is for vehicles that are unable to cross a small arroyo (one mile prior to the trailhead), and the second is at the trailhead itself. The hike begins at the second trailhead.

Jackrabbit

Trail 12A: Cinco Tinajas – 3.0 Mile Loop

Cinco Tinajas Trail

Trail Highlights

One of the most popular trails in the park interior because of its accessibility and fabulous attractions, including: pre-historic pictographs (rock art); panoramic views from the overlook; and the five naturally formed rock pools, known as "tinajas."

We provide two options for this hike:

- **Trail 12A:** An easy-to-moderate 3.0 mile hike including all attractions.
- **Trail 12B:** A 1.0 mile hike visiting the scenic overlook and the naturally formed rock pools, known as "tinajas".

CAUTION: Flash flooding is possible in this area. Do not enter Leyva Creek, Sauceda Creek, or visit the tinajas if it has rained or if rain is expected. Check with a Park Ranger regarding conditions.

Approximate Distance:	3.0 miles
Difficulty:	Easy to moderate
Trail Surface:	Rock and sand
Estimated Time:	1.5 – 2.0 hours
Trail Usage:	Hiking, Equestrian

The Hike and Trail – Pour-off, Rock Art, Scenic Overlook, and Tinajas

The trail starts in the parking area, just behind the trailhead sign and map. Follow the trail for 0.25 miles, heading north and reaching a trail intersection with an option to turn right to hike along the ridgeline.

Continue straight (north) for an additional 0.25 miles, hiking down the fairly steep, rocky trail to the bottom of the hill and creek bed. Make a mental note of the rock cairn indicating the junction of the trail where it joins the creek bed. This is an important marker for your return journey.

Turn right, heading along the creek bed for approximately 200 yards until reaching the canyon walls and pour-off. The erosion in the canyon walls provides a great view of the pour-off and of the steep, smooth canyon walls carved by the flow of rushing water.

Walk back along the creek bed for 0.25 miles, passing by the rock cairn on the left-hand side where you previously entered the creek bed. At the junction of two branches of Leyva Creek, turn right (east) up Leyva Creek for 0.3 miles following rock cairns and keeping an eye out for a group of large boulders on the hillside to your left. At 1.3 miles (total distance from trailhead) you will now be able to see a series of boulders on a hill to your left, and a rock cairn

Pour-off below Scenic Overlook

leading to a cattle trail. Turn left (north) and head toward the boulders on the hillside, following the cattle trail and rock cairns through the creosote bushes.

The archeological site containing prehistoric pictographs (rock art) is under an overhang on the large boulder to the far left, at the base of the hill. The rock art is fragile, so please don't touch it. To the right of the rock art, you can also visit a shelter with a circular depression in the rock that was used by people in the past to crush and grind plants.

After admiring the rock art and shelter, return along the original cattle trail to Levya Creek. Turn right while retracing your steps to the intersection in approximately 0.3 miles. Turn left (south), and hike along the original creek bed toward the pour-off, looking for the rock cairn and the trail where you originally entered the creek bed.

Rock Art (Pictographs)

Turn right and follow the trail up the short hill for approximately 0.25 miles. As you approach the top of the hill, look for a trail junction with a trail bordered by rocks on the left-hand side.

Turn left (east), following the trail along the ridgeline for approximately 300 yards to the overlook. [*Alternatively*, continue straight and return to the parking area.]

The overlook provides spectacular views of the surrounding mountains including Oso Peak to the southwest (the highest point in the Park), La Mota Mesa to the north, and Cerro Boludo to the south.

From the overlook, return along the same trail for approximately 100 yards, reaching a trail junction marked by rock cairns. Turn left, initially heading southwest and following the rock cairns down the gentle slope to the creek. Pass through the creek and continue over the historic rock wall until you see the tinajas on your left.

The tinajas and rock walls are very slippery, especially after rain, so use caution and never go down a pour-off that you cannot climb out of.

Note: It is against state park regulations to swim in a tinajas. Wildlife use the water for survival and it must not be contaminated by humans.

To return to the parking area and trailhead, turn around and retrace your steps over the historic rock wall and continue along the creek bed until you reach the Main Park Road in 0.3 miles. Turn right, and the parking area will be a short walk to the right.

Approximate Distance	Reference Points for Trail 12 A
0.25 miles	Parking area to trail intersection (north). Continue straight (heading down the steep, rocky hill).
0.5 miles	Reach creek bed. Turn right.
0.7 miles	Reach the pour-off. Return along the creek.
1.0 miles	Reach the Levya Creek intersection. Turn right.
1.3 miles	Look for large boulders on the hillside to the left and a rock cairn. Turn left, following a trail through the creosote bushes toward the boulders.
1.32 miles	Reach the rock art located on a boulder on the far left at the bottom of the hill.
1.34 miles	Return to the Leyva Creek bed. Turn right, and retrace your steps to the intersection.
1.65 miles	Turn left, heading back toward the pour-off along the original creek bed.
1.7 miles	Turn right at the rock cairn (where you originally entered the creek) and hike up the hill.
2.0 miles	Reach trail junction toward the top of the hill. Turn left (east) and follow the trail along the ridgeline toward the overlook. [*Alternatively*, continue straight and return to the parking area and trailhead.]
2.2 miles	Reach the overlook with a great view of the surrounding mountains. Retrace your steps for approximately 100 yards to a trail junction on your left.
2.25 miles	Turn left, heading southwest, gently traversing down the lava rock toward the creek.
2.5 miles	Cross the creek. Proceed over the historic rock wall.
2.6 miles	Reach the tinajas on your left. This is also the turnaround point. Hike back over the rock wall and along the creek heading south until you reach the Main Park Road.
2.95 miles	Reach the Main Park Road. Turn right.
3.0 miles	Arrive back at the parking area and trailhead.

- Please do not touch the prehistoric pictographs (rock art). Photos are allowed.

- Smooth rocks around the tinajas are very slippery when wet; use caution.

- Don't climb down anything you can't get back up.

- Swimming in the tinajas is against park regulations.

- Sunset is a great time to visit.

- Leyva Escondido Spring is 0.3 miles east of the rock art along the creek bed and is easily identified by the cluster of green Cottonwood trees. Typically, it is not possible to see water as the spring is underground. If you reach the Springs before finding the cattle trail leading to the rock art you have gone too far.

Finding the Trailhead

From the Sauceda Ranger Station drive 1.3 miles west to the Cinco Tinajas parking area on your right.

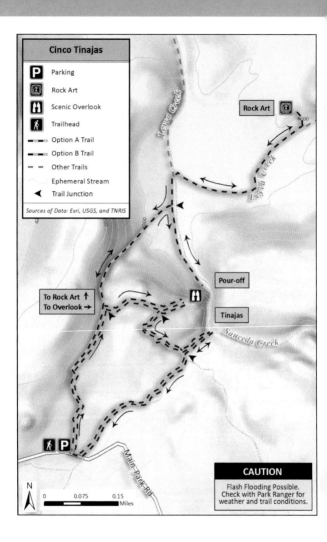

Cinco Tinajas

P	Parking
🖼	Rock Art
🚻	Scenic Overlook
🚶	Trailhead
▬ ▬	Option A Trail
▬ ▬	Option B Trail
- -	Other Trails
	Ephemeral Stream
◄	Trail Junction

Sources of Data: Esri, USGS, and TNRIS

Laguna Creek

Rock Art 🖼

Laguna Creek

Pour-off

🚻

To Rock Art ↑
To Overlook →

Tinajas

Sauceda Creek

🚶 **P**

Main Park Rd

N

0   0.075   0.15
Miles

CAUTION

Flash Flooding Possible.
Check with Park Ranger for
weather and trail conditions.

Trail 12B: Cinco Tinajas – 1.0 Mile Loop

Tinajas

Trail Highlights

Trail B: An easy 1.0-mile hike visiting the five naturally formed rock pools known as "tinajas" and the scenic over-look with panoramic views of the surrounding mountains.

> **CAUTION:** Flash flooding is possible in this area. Do not enter Leyva Creek, Sauceda Creek, or visit the tinajas if it has rained or if rain is expected. Check with a Park Ranger regarding conditions.

Approximate Distance:	1.0 mile
Difficulty:	Easy
Trail Surface:	Rock and sand
Estimated Time:	45 – 60 minutes
Trail Usage:	Hiking, Equestrian

The Hike and Trail – Scenic Overlook and Tinajas

The trail starts in the parking area, just behind the trail-head sign and map. Follow the trail for 0.25 miles heading north and reaching a trail intersection. Turn right (east) and follow the trail along the ridgeline bordered by rocks for approximately 300 yards to the overlook.

The overlook provides spectacular views of the surrounding mountains, including Oso Peak to the southwest (the highest point in the Park), La Mota Mesa to the north, and Cerro Boludo to the south.

From the overlook, return along the same trail for approximately 100 yards, reaching a trail junction marked by rock cairns. Turn left, initially heading southwest and following the rock cairns down the gentle slope to the creek. Pass through the creek and continue over the historic rock wall until you see the tinajas on your left.

Note: It is against state park regulations to swim in a tinajas. Wildlife use the water for survival and it must not be contaminated by humans.

To return to the parking area and trailhead, turn around and retrace your steps over the historic rock wall and continue along the creek bed until you reach the Main Park Road in 0.3 miles. Turn right, and the parking area will be a short walk to the right.

See Trail Map on Page 76. Follow Option B (blue trail).

Approximate Distance	Reference Points for Trail 12 B
0.25 miles	Parking area to trail intersection (north). Turn right (east), following the trail along the ridgeline.
0.4 miles	Reach the overlook with a great view of the surrounding mountains. Retrace your steps for approximately 100 yards to a trail junction on your left.
0.45 miles	Turn left, heading southwest, gently traversing down the lava rock toward the creek.
0.5 miles	Cross the creek and proceed over the historic rock wall.
0.7 miles	Reach the tinajas on your left. This is also the turnaround point. Hike back over the rock wall and along the creek heading south until you reach the Main Park Road.
1.0 miles	Reach the Main Park Road. Turn right.
1.05 miles	Arrive back at the parking area and trailhead.

Tips

- Smooth rocks around the tinajas are very slippery when wet; use caution.

- Don't climb down a rock wall of pour-off if it will be a challenge to climb back up.

- Swimming in the tinajas is against park regulations.

- Sunset is a great time to visit.

INTERESTING FACT

Tinajas is a Spanish word for desert water basins carved into bedrock by the erosive force of sand, gravel, and stones suspended by rushing water.

The trail is named "Cinco Tinajas" as five tinajas can be seen along the trail.

Finding the Trailhead

From the Sauceda Ranger Station drive 1.3 miles west to the Cinco Tinajas parking area on your right.

About the Authors

Robert and Jenny Fuller

Robert and Jenny are passionate adventure travelers with a love for the great outdoors. They embrace an active lifestyle and enjoy visiting unique destinations, away from large cities and big crowds. For the last two decades they have traveled extensively throughout North and South America, Europe, and Australia combining their passion for hiking and experiencing local cultures.

As residents of Texas they visit and camp frequently at Texas State Parks and enjoy the wonderful hiking trails and services provided.

The core principal guiding Robert and Jenny to create a series of trail guides was to enhance the hiker's experience on the trail and to give back by donating 50% of Half Day Hikes' proceeds from the sale of each guidebook. This book was written to support Big Bend Ranch State Park and Texas Parks and Wildlife's mission.

Robert and Jenny are members of the Texas Parks & Wildlife Foundation, Texans for State Parks, Texas State Historical Association, the Audubon Society, and are Legacy Members of the Nature Conservancy.

Texas Parks & Wildlife's Mission
"To manage and conserve the natural and cultural resources of Texas, and to provide hunting, fishing, and outdoor recreation opportunities for the use and enjoyment of present and future generations."

Glossary & Terms

Arroyo: Dry creek or stream bed which temporarily or seasonally fills and flows with water.

Caldera: Large volcanic crater, typically formed by a major eruption leading to the collapse of the mouth of the volcano.

Candelilla: A small shrub found in northern Mexico and the southwestern United States. Candelilla wax is derived from the leaves of the Candelilla shrub and can be found in candles, lip balm, crayons, and chewing gum. Candelilla means "little candle" in Spanish.

Cinnabar: Cinnabar, or mercury sulfide (HgS), is a highly toxic, naturally occurring form of the mercury mineral. It was used in the past for producing a bright orange pigment on ceramics, murals, and tattoos.

Conglomerate Rock: Conglomerate is a sedimentary rock made of rounded pebbles and sand that is usually held together (cemented) by silica, calcite or iron oxide. It is similar to sandstone, but the rock particles are rounded or angular gravel, rather than sand.

Ephemeral Stream: A stream that is typically dry and only flows during and shortly after a period of rainfall.

Hoodoo: Weathered rock with an interesting shape, mainly found in the desert. Hoodoos typically consist of relatively soft rock (tuff or mudstone) topped by harder, less easily eroded stone. Example on Page 11.

Laccolith: Mass of igneous rock, typically lens-shaped that has been intruded between rock strata, causing uplift in the shape of a dome.

Pour-off: Desert waterfall that is only active after substantial rains. Example on Page 17 (Closed Canyon) & Page 71 (Cinco Tinajas).

Riparian Zone: An ecosystem that lies between land and water, where water-dependent plants and animals live and thrive. They are diverse and can be small areas by streams, creeks, or larger areas by major rivers or water bodies. Example on Page 51 (Ojito Adentro).

Rock Basket: A stack of rocks typically contained in a wire basket with a trail sign or arrow.

Rock Cairn: A vertical stack of rocks organized to indicate trail direction.

Seep: Where water flows or oozes gradually through a porous substance. While Ojito Adentro is officially referred to as a waterfall, you will typically just see water seeping from the rocks. Example on Page 51.

Slot Canyon: A long, narrow, deep, and tortuous channel or drainage way with sheer rock walls that is subject to flash flooding. A slot canyon is significantly deeper than it is wide. Example on Page 15 (Closed Canyon).

Welded Tuff: A type of rock that, when hot enough, will weld together at the time of deposition.

Trail Descriptions

Loop Trail: Trail or combination of trails that return to the original starting point.

Out and Back: One-way trail on which you travel to a destination, then backtrack to the original trailhead.

Trail Connector: A trail that connects one trail or several trails to return the hiker to the original starting point.

Trail Junction: The intersection of two or more trails.

Made in the USA
Coppell, TX
06 December 2019